UNCHARTED

UNCHARTED

SABYASACHI NAG

Mansfield Press

Library and Archives Canada Cataloguing in Publication

Title: Uncharted / Sabyasachi Nag.
Names: Nag, Sabyasachi, 1968- author.
Description: Poems.
Identifiers: Canadiana 20200372114 | ISBN 9781771262484 (softcover)
Classification: LCC PS8627.A483 U73 2020 | DDC C811/.6—dc23

Editor for the press: Stuart Ross
Typesetting & Cover Design: Denis De Klerck

The publication of *Uncharted* has been generously supported by
the Canada Council for the Arts and the Ontario Arts Council.

Mansfield Press Inc.
25 Mansfield Avenue, Toronto, Ontario, Canada M6J 2A9
Publisher: Denis De Klerck
www.mansfieldpress.net

for Junaid Khan (2003–2018)
nunquam obliteratus

CONTENTS

III. DEATH

I. IDENTITY

MARIA AFTER THE CONCERT

Back home, after a quiet week at work,
when she opened the door,
I leaned over to touch a speck
of pixie glitter on her collarbone.
After dinner, her blood pressure rose.
She needed a rub on her shoulders
before she could breathe properly.
It was Friday.
We changed into pink night clothes –
a kind of foreplay
before a series of open-heart surgeries.
On TV, experts were analyzing
Japanese bush warbler songs
and how the city birds
with more complex song structure
were guaranteed better sex
and longer lives.
This was followed by images
of Salman Abedi;
bobbies on Brandt Street, talking;
Ariana Grande pouting at cameras
before the Manchester concert;
all of this while she lay
curled on my thighs
like a piece of cashmere.
The bronze skin of her nape, red
from absent-minded stroking
frozen in time.
Suddenly, she started dissolving
in a pool of paraffin –
first her head, then features on her face,
arms, spine, the toned muscles of her calf –
reflecting the darkness that huddled
around us, in the room.

When she came back to form,
she was charging around
the breadth of the flat –
a wretched half demon,
just out from radiation –
fearing, she will be told, they failed
to take the tumour off her throat.
She almost knocked the TV,
where the topic had changed –
they were discussing the benefits
of donkey milk soap.
I tried coaxing her into the bath,
washing her head, fixing a drink.
Forgetting won't change anything, she said.

WHAT WE MAKE OF SYMBOLS

One bone-cold Sunday night,
flipping raw photos from a recent trip,
we stopped by a yellow taxi
in Calcutta.

Shirtless boys, my son's age,
the white of their teeth luminous in the dark,
noses pressed to the glass of the rained afternoon,
were begging for food.

One of them in the far corner of the frame
looked away from us all, woozily
drawing vapour swastikas
on the fog of his breath;

same as my son on the frost of the window –
his newcomer's eyes looking out
into frozen yards, blinking red, green, gold;
elves riding reindeers on fire.

DEALING WITH THE WITNESSES
after James Tate

We were new to the neighbourhood
and still opening doors to strangers,
when they came in their grey coats –
man and wife. Witnesses.
On their way in, they pointed at the winter
charred lime and chili totem
threaded in a red string to the door frame.

Oh, those! I scratched my head
in embarrassment, made something up:
Seven veils around the soul.
And it's only the skin that darkens with time.
Inside, acids that keep the skinks out
also gnaw down the arteries to heaven
and all that's left of the storm is the shell
glowing in the dark, like a chime
around the void.

But those are only just three chilies
and a lime, the man protested,
displaying anger, disbelief.

Others must have fallen to the ground,
eaten away by lizards, squirrels, moths –
taken by the wind.

That's a lie.
Don't you listen to him, sir,
my wife interjected,
coldly giving me away.

Oh! Hands on chest,
the witnesses gasped.
They are really decoys, she went on,
meant to propitiate the goddess of bad luck
right out the door.

And they looked back at her speechless,
as though that scared them
even more.

CROUCHING CAVEMAN HIDDEN CELLAR

At the museum I met an artist I knew.
Have you seen him? he said.
Who?
The caveman, he said.
What caveman?

The one who lives inside your cellar
and paints your interior walls;
walls, doors, fences inked on his forearms;
bunch of used locks dangling down his earlobes;
the guy with the RESPECT undershirt.

What's he doing here? I asked.

Eyes on everyone else, hungry for battle,
he's searching the smallest shadow
– doubt, disrespect, detachment;
eyes so large they look like craters
in a cave wall, facing other cavemen.

I have never seen him, I said.

When I brought it up with my doctor,
he pointed at the bench and fished out a helix.
That's actually an apparition.
What triggers it is this gene here.
Like dopamine, it can give you a high.
The almost burn, the almost ecstasy,
you feel in and outside your arteries,
walking the dirt path where you first kissed –
places you were born, teats you suckled –
that's not your soul suddenly stirring out of turn,
not even consciousness;
that's the caveman squatting on his haunches
calling you.

After so much medication,
how can that be? I wanted to ask.
The lady at the Hypnosis Store
pointed to the recliner, fired up incense,
put on Marconi Union on LP.
Look, there's a rainbow over your head,
she said, pointing at the window.
Do you see it?
Now let's crawl into the cellar.
Follow me. Don't make a sound.
Now you are in the cellar.
Do you see the caveman crouched in half-lotus?
Do you see light streaming out his mouth?
Now push the door gently.
Show respect, he will let you in.
Down the stairwell, see that?
A whole new world –
bread, music, myth, history,
honey-fattened figs, soaked in opium;
do you smell the myrrh?

Exhausted.
On the last train home,
I looked into the fade of twilight,
into suburban backyards – discarded toys,
hooded barbecues, bric-a-brac;
skies darkening; clouds gathering;
the window flipping over
to reveal a translucent portrait of me
looking into a mirror.
I looked again. Oh yes. There,
the rainbow over my head.
My red eyes popped wide like caveman eyes,
straight out and never blinking;

mouth slightly open, reflecting light.
I opened my mouth wider, wider.
I tried reaching the cellar with my tongue.
Down the stairwell I could sense someone crouched.
Someone waiting to be found; touched.

SONG OF AYLAN

Three columns of scratches on the Ishango bone.
Forty nights of rain, one lost sheep and ninety-nine remaining;
thirteen heads on the hill, four bellies in the cow, that's the song of Aylan.

Only in middle school are you so sure about numbers.
Uncertainty is both dragon and phoenix – seven types of doubt? Eighteen
shades of skin? Half a million dead make the song of Aylan.

In Egypt: number ten: a rope; hundred: a coil of ropes; thousand: a lotus;
ten thousand: wives, concubines; one million prisoners.
The chant of colliding atoms is the song of Aylan.

In Syria: ten million: refugees; in the heart of sky, a billion
years before the sun will die. Who needs numbers? Why must we testify?
We got here before we got lost; tall mast and a star – in the song of Aylan.

Perhaps there are patterns in the sky beyond the sieve of language.
Perhaps gods float on holograms; perhaps it's plain kismet
we learned to count the dead before we learned the song of Aylan.

Maybe we will find our passage through time someday.
Maybe we will find eight ways to swim the seas someday.
Three days in the belly of fish; twelve ways to teach the song of Aylan.

Maybe the blue curve will bend someday, maybe Saturn will come home.
Maybe someday in the shadow of Yggdrasil.
Maybe with the fog of our breath we shall remake the song of Aylan.

Maybe the eye will open to new ways of seeing.
Maybe new songs won't impose beat over melody. Maybe
we shall meet again by the sea, bent over like Aylan, dreaming.

ODE TO FISHING

All day I am at the pier watching this kid
shake down the rod, stick bait,
reel the line before arching
the small of his back to cast farther and farther –

What kind of fish
would show up in such shallows?

The strong, bulbous water hyacinth
inquire differently – how does one grow roots,
without dirt, just by floating?
What does one know of arrivals?
What do we leave when we leave home?

When our eyes meet, this kid and I –
we are strangers, we carry on,
away from the streets; from cars, buskers, carousels;
a crowd's milling around;
in minutes another year will turn.

Breathing through eyes
is a way of the wolf,
another year of empty chase.
Who do we owe?

How much beauty do we need?
How much deeper into the earth must we travel?
How much farther from home
before we have truly arrived? Departed?

Among friends, under the neon the kid is no longer
the stranger baiting in the dark – he is more sure.
He inquires differently – eyes trenched narrow.
How does anyone know what to follow?
When's it late too late to turn around?

Maybe fishing is a kind of forfeiting.
Maybe forfeiting is a kind of arriving.
Maybe arriving is a kind of growing roots in water,
without dirt, like shapeless fish shadows
moving elsewhere.

CARRYING A BOMB IN THE BRAIN

In the college housing
firemen went about their jobs, searching
for a bomb someone reported.

In their high boots, orange uniform,
hard tools of trade hanging from their waist,
if they were scared, you couldn't tell

from the way they talked –
reflectors bursting like stars in the outer galaxy –
they stopped occasionally to look,
as if they were immortal;
or they had access to a higher truth.

Out on a park bench, wardens
with flags and megaphones gathered
to shout out instructions –
see something, say something.

Before they said it was a hoax
and the firemen left, something else took over –
a wild seizure of straw blaze
and in the hollow of the chest

not fear.
Or maybe it was the loony fear
of a bomb actually hiding among us all,
all wired and hidden inside a brain.

The street,
teeming with black and white heads;
the windows shimmied as we looked up
angry, anxious, then drained.

ODE ELSEWHERE

If dying is what we know it is –
period of the wave – what use is history?
Men defeating men. Men surviving men,
a game of poker.

If you look out the window and yell,
you know the sky will stop right before your eyes.
If you stop by the edge of darkness,
you know the wild will come closer.

If you stab your arteries, you know blood will become copper.
When you hear birdsong, you know eyes are not for seeing.
When you hear the woods, you know the length of shadow.
But what should I say to my son?

Looking back at the trail, should I say: be a tree,
because home is a real place and returning
is how you repay the ground you stand on? Or should I say:
be a leaf – it doesn't matter what you believe.

MY GRANDMA'S VIRGIN

My grandma's long straight hair was tonsured
when she lost her husband to TB at sixteen.
No one asked. It was simply the serrated wheel, turning.

Watching men in temple courtyards running the ustura's blade
in short, precise strokes on the dripping velvet scalp,
seems a religious act. My grandma's act of religion –

perhaps, in equal measures a conscious channelling of grief
and subconscious channelling of capital
into systems best preserved when separated from reason.

Like the aspen shining even when the sun is hidden or the maple –
with no timetables, teachers, no apparent memory of spring –
knowing enough to relinquish everything when it's time.

And reason is almost weightless when knowing matters less
than being the sixteen-year-old daughter, getting a weft
at Hair Priestess off the hill. Her pick: velvet Peruvian virgin.

What happened to her long dark weave? My grandma
didn't care to look back or know. All she remembered
was how the head felt after. Lighter? Weighted down?

My daughter sucks in her cheeks and nods in disbelief.
You can't feel them. You can't even tell it's there/not there.
Lighter than the breeze flowing on corn, ready for harvest.

CATASTROPHE THAT NEARLY BROUGHT DOWN A PLANE

After late-night Li Bo,
on a plane to Houston, out of sheer intumescence
I begin unravelling a sickness bag –
starting with the wired throat,
then the pleated sides, then bottom.
My finger trapezing through the waxed paper
feels like a tall-masted skiff – almost Odysseus,
slicing Lake Ontario: placid like an eye
that has seen without knowing –
seen earth before there was blood,
before the peach blossoms, before words –
midsummer sky like cut nectarine –
before butterflies; moon rivers; temple bells.

Meanwhile, in the seat behind me
someone's talking out loud.
His language of gestures and force – lost
on everyone, like some forgotten folklore.
Bloodshot, stubble-faced, his unbuttoned shirt
resting on his chest in reverse
like a deflated child suckling a mother's hairy teat.
He tamps down the child and talks
to the young girl beside him,
to the men in front of him.
The girl is anxious, can't understand a thing.
She has nowhere to go.
Hasn't heard anyone talk like this before.
Not rant, not even sermon, just talk – modulated
like rain gurgling down tin eaves – incessant,
torrential rain, pointing to a whole universe
outside sealed plastic windows.
Folks that have spent their entire lives looking away
have to stretch their necks hard, looking for him –
the man who won't stop talking.

Anxious attendants scurry up and down the aisle
begging the man to stop.
Stop. Stop. Stop.
Facing the girl, he ignores them all, as though
he has been *alone under the moon, drinking,*
after being forced to shut up too long.

HOW TO INTERPRET A DREAM

Look here, the officer said, pointing
at the instrument firing X-rays
into my brown heart. Then he got busy
matching fingerprints to felons, no-fliers.
As the red laser cut through my skin
Try again, he said.
Touch your finger to the tongue.
Flipping pages on my blue passport,
he stopped where my six-year-old had drawn
a scurry of scarlet patterns.
What are these? he asked.

Goldfish and Octopus, I said.
They lived with us inside a bell jar
above the fireplace.
You could see the goldfish, not the octopus,
before they hit the glass of the bell jar,
both of them at once;
or maybe the goldfish first,
one fine morning, out of nowhere,
as though something in their brains boiled
over and they were done
doing what they were told.

And? the officer asked, brow cocked.

As the jar tipped, the Goldfish
danced itself to death and the Octopus
appeared from nowhere, stretching
itself, past the scattered glass;
stretching into a river of sorts –
a locked river inside a locked room, bleeding
where the sun scraped the skin.

Because a room is no place for a river
octopus, floating like a sea anemone –
shiny, colourless, shifting, weightless –
even though it was gathering in places,
metaphors way outside its own weight,
and because it happened really quickly –
like an ancient apparition, you know,
not from seeing but instinct –
it had to be preserved
here, in the book of passage, and erasures.

WAR STORY

Rebels across the street
stole apples. Now they have
got hold of a gun.

                               Five have come back fallen
                         wrapped in flags between Super-
                                    bowl commercials.

Met says: effects of El Niño
have been so devastating,
there shall be no rain.

                         A temple was defiled with animal
                          dung, another desecrated
                                  with girlhood.

Rebels who stole apples
are now friends with predators
that stole peaches and destroyed the garden.

                         Clergymen grooming boys.
                              Boys grooming
                             to become clergy.

Cow skinners,
corpse beaters,
rag pickers,
rat killers,
crushed-bottle collectors,
knife grinders found –
packed like matchsticks
inside a book.

                                    The cattle buried
                              under scorched earth
                                     a heap of ash.

Razorbacks have planted a flag
with one pole that flies
our pennant.

                                       Glaciers wait
                                     for the rivers
                                 to flow backwards.

Grandpa stole cheese. Bees were asleep.
Bees stole the cheese back after Grandpa died.
What happened in history isn't all the history.

                  Everyone has something unfinished.
                                          It's normal
                                  to demand respect.

HISTORY LESSON AT SCHOOL

In the museum of civilizations when we passed
by the hall fitted with excavated mirrors
and shiny headphones playing back,
in all major languages, trench talk from
forgotten wars, our teacher said, *Here* –
let me show you how to hold time.
We laughed, as if it were even possible to have
air trapped inside history.

He led us to a bathhouse around the block,
abandoned and its walls thick with algae.
Get naked, he said.
Down to your boxers, everyone.
Now throw your arms around,
you lazy rascals, he said.
Paddle as though you were drowning.
Now raise your face in slow motion.
Breathe! At the top of his lungs, he yelled
at Dip, my cousin, forever slow to catch on
to new ways of doing things.

Then he made us duck under imagined waves.
High as windmills.
High as windmills, he repeated
Do you hear the wheel of time
crushing dead leaves? he asked,
looking straight into Dip's disbelieving heart.
What about lizards trapped inside bubbles?
Do you see them, scared by their own reflection?

The fish, the snails, the leaves, the larvae?
Do you feel the unguent crawling out of your ears?
Down again, he said, and we kept repeating,
until we could take it no more, and lied.

Yes. Yes. We see it. We hear it –
we shall not forget, in chorus we said,
singing the space between our ears, before
quietly returning to the dank of grade-school math;
back to the filaments of spirogyra;
back to elements of Euclid; chemistry of tin.

ODE TO THEM

1

Who are they?
my ten-year-old asks.
I almost run them over,
the new folks from wars abroad,
as they shuffle in muslin scarves.

Why now?
I turn around to ask –
K-pop unfolding on his phone
between hot flashes of confederacy wars
in faraway Charlottesville, 2017 –
torn skin bandaged in stars
float on the glass, curved like clouds;
blood on asphalt, cured in rain.

2

We stop over for doughnuts.

3

Everyone rushes out of the chapel.
It's claustrophobic.
Soon there will be speeches; ceremony;
my son has questioned everyone.
Who are they?

4

Back when we were refugees
flooding another border elsewhere,
there were those who'd keep vigil

by the jambed door, afraid
we would draw them into our despair
between our lava eyes –

and they wouldn't let us sing –
some of us had deep voices those days –
deep like wheat coming out of dirt,
covered in dead leaves
over corpses put down in haste –

and they won't let us work –
and some of us had good hands in those days –
hands that could bake bricks in the kiln
of our cinnamon chest, caved,
as if it were a wound, waiting.

Our chests glowed as we pulled
hard on those narrow cigarillos.
Don't touch,
they'd spit to our face
as we bristled out of hiding, like ants, dressed up
after a hurried prayer –

vassal ants following the scent of sugar cherubs,
sugar angels, sugar gods.
We were hungry.
We were quick.
We'd eat anything.

5

Don't touch,
we would spit back to the face
of those who got too close
with hands and implements,
shadows bent in the sun like medieval shoes.

6

Don't touch,
we would spit back to the face
of the brother and butcher –
back then, the only butcher left on our street –
the butcher who stayed –

stunned in the act of sliding his hands
away from the flowers –
lily and tube rose – threaded
into rings for dead gods,
ancestors.

The only butcher on our street –
he could dunk the meat in a tote
without looking – his art.

7

Enough! I say.
Let's get dessert.

REMEDIES FOR TEREUSITIS

Certain alpha hoopoes have the taste
for both, Philomel and Itys.
Elsewhere, they hunt after dark when exhaust
from the beer factory gags the sky so tight
one can taste the malt in their wing pits.
Gods know. They respond by reforming
believers into nightingales, swallows.
Then they take a break from trying.
Conjure a new Ovid, request new hosannas.

Certain ranting rebel birds
they reconfigure into line-following photovores
you find clinging to guardrails
or reflected on neo-colonial candelabra –
their muscles pumped with plastic blood
programmed to put them in auto-reverse
soon as they hit a wall.
Then they make walls.

Then they take down the lights. Observe –
in meditative half-lotus, half-closed eyes.
Those that repeat-fail clearly laid rules,
they transform them into fire ants
you find after a storm has warped the steel,
taken everything.
Their arteries choked with moon lather
that would put them on burn
soon as someone touches them.

MIRRORS ARE FOR DWARFS

In our colony of Gigantopithecus apes,
when it became evident –
after years of genuflecting to the slow drawl
of priests, politicians, ascetics, and evangelicals –
our spines knotted; our waists unresponsive
to even the slightest requirement for locomotion;
hearts deposited with the family gold
in deep vaults; lungs syndicated
without anyone ever paying attention –
elders had to call a meeting.

Dressed like farmers,
beagles, ale drapers, astronomers,
besom makers, abecedarians, journeymen,
we assembled with festoons
and message boards saved
from the last big assembly, expecting
first to be fed and feted,
then told.

Enough!
Do something, the elders demanded.
Everything recycles in time, someone retorted.
What about them dwarfs?
someone asked – someone with an inborn
proclivity for asking the wrong question
at the wrong time –
What about them?

Dwarfs in alien systems
spend their whole miserable lives
eating, pooping, procreating;
they have no time for reflection,
said the Chief of Eugenics.

Sure as hell,
the elders wanted a different answer
or the same sucker shit spun differently –
they had him escorted out
before addressing the crowd.
Don't listen to him.

What now? the crowd demanded.

Take down the mirrors, an elder said.
Every twisted mirror from our land of
absolute, unmitigated, bountiful greatness.
No prisoners. No witnesses.
Not a trace to be left behind.
Do it as if earth had been invaded
by an army of carping revenants
and this one trick would save us all.

What about us?
the mirror makers howled back.
Don't we have debts, mortgages,
mouths to feed?

Down you take them, you imbecile –
mirrors from walls, here in the upper world,
to have them hung back on them dwarfs–
walls, ceilings, floors, crevices, caves;
mirrors like barnacles; screw them in,
any dank place that would take a fucking nail.

What would that do?
the hammer makers asked.

Everyone kept silent, unsure –
sympathizing with each other's slowness
in the uptake of the deeper nuances;

gloating in the fuzz of reflected genius;
others laughed as loud as they could,
dreaming up in their minds
alien dwarfs going nuts
looking at themselves in mirrors –
cheeks sucked in, lips bloated, duck-faced.
They knew already,
they were going to win this one.

THE FACT OF THE DOOR

At the steel mill, the empty hallway
closed on one end; on the other end a door –
always shut.

Sometimes it crept out of frame and walked,
as I walked, among shadows of winter-dead
chrysanthemum. It was December.

Ghosts or shadows or racks of false portraiture:
who knew what key could unlock its soul –
a loud explosion, or arias imported from Paestum.

The warp of cured metal woven under layers
of discarded skin – the door never swung,
never slammed, never betrayed its dark occult.

Unmoving witness, destined to outlast us all;
even the graffiti chiselled in bold-black says
history has been here before.

Sometimes I'd stand in awe, as if it were mountain.
Sometimes I'd listen beneath, as if it were tree.
Sometimes I would taste the dark river.

Ghosts or actors, I could hear them laugh inside,
and I laughed with them. When the laughing stopped,
beyond the crabgrass there, you could see the ocean.

HOW TO RAISE THEM IN MOSS PARK

You sit with a counsellor sipping cheap Chardonnay.
Soon the cup is empty and her cardinal-red lip stain
on the glass rim remains, each line distinct like a flute
feeding a choked estuary – you suppose
because she hasn't spoken a word since you ranted
about raising kids here in Moss Park.

Meanwhile addicts, twitching in withdrawal,
take turns hand-selling a bag
of summer gowns, pop tags intact.
A girl in a misshapen blouse is slouched
by a *Homeless* sign stood up against
an orange witch hat, a yellow lab by her feet.

Way before they can stand up straight, she said –
drowning out the cars and construction drill –
before they walk past the sorority years
in cheerleaders' uniforms, licking the afternoon glacé;
before they bear the cross of your meaning;
before they become the reason, the whole idea,
the song in its entirety – that's when they are perfect.

You shake your head in disbelief.
How could your blood become the bitch?
Go away. Get the fuck out.
That's all you hear. That's all they want.
And reduced, redacted, you sway out
or drop down on your knees, begging for a piece
of the dirt to squeeze up close and dream
from the same dark space
as you once did,
together.
What a scandal!
You say that without pausing to breathe.

Everyone's entitled to their one private Hiroshima,
she said. *Yet, when the jury is off radar*
and truth can take off in a thick mushroom taxi –
and it's OK to stay back in town
with the pumice stone of your own failed history –
like the lip stain on the rim of a wine-washed glass –
you have no use for guilt, blame, denial, regret.

In which case – what is the question?
What good is Kant?
If that's what you want to know –
if you haven't triumphed and you have busted
your ass trying, trying – remember this:
when does raising ever end?
She says that and leaves the curb by the arena,
now thick with dealers and pimps.

FIELD NOTES FROM THE JOB FAIR

Red stripes on hard-boiled candies
converge in a feverish dance
inside the polished glass jar at the job fair hotel.
Chrome shines through thumbprints.
There is more coffee in tall flasks.

The telephone rings again, rings, then stops.
Snow piles on railing caps.
Applicants for the new factory have left
their trail deep into the brick carpet.
The last applicant holds a bouquet, awaiting a ride.

With a handful of nubbins under bell sleeves,
placed in plain sight, she is trying to return
from nursing her mother who died
last month from tumours in the intestine.

Pausing for words, as though she were picking
them out from an unclear stream, she confesses
she hasn't talked to anyone in a while.
But what do confessions count, in this job
inserting hubcaps on a stone-still wheel?

In her eyes you see the craquelure.
She says she got too close to death to be idle
emptying out, as though she were starting
fresh from a bone flush and her hands are trained
cradling the gurney, shooting insulin.

Lovely, she says, at the end of the silence –
pointing at the bouquet of pink
hydrangeas, beargrass and aspidistra.
Would you like to have it? someone offers.

Blood rushes her pale-as-blue-milk face –
veins lit up like lightning
between the ridges of her high cheeks.
She pauses for a moment, as if considering
the arrangement again, before
letting her eyes dance just a little bit.

ODE TO YOUNG POETS AT A SUNDAY READING

I know poets gassed inside the kitchen,
white towels tucked under doors;
or out in the wild, drinking
from Dionysian cups; drowned in Spezia;
I know them chained at a train station,
lynched with the spit of homophobia –
what death can't take is staggering;
what we fear is coded in our minds –

said a dead laureate's son at a Sunday reading,
pointing at the far corner
of the Central Library – his own books
autographed and delicately arranged,
shiny, like just-washed hair, waiting to be touched.
Listen up – he went on, the strums on his guitar
climbing: A minor to G major
as if the power were out
and he knew of a fire in the basement
climbing up the stairs.

Someone read from a manuscript:
killing Caesar again in broad daylight,
right by the atrium, no one caring
to take note of the senators who'd stayed back
after the daggers had left the general's body –
limp and open like a sunflower after a storm.
Someone else staged an echolalia –
yes, no, yes, no, yes.

Outside, it snowed unseasonally. Still April –
as the crowd dwindled down to the librarian's assistant
and a few young poets awaited
their chance at the open mic.
The damp sun dabbed the high windows with a damp cloth,

the hesitant glide of vowels easily outplayed
by the murmur of fluorescents
shining on empty chairs.

They seemed immortal –
young poets shuffling like loyal senators
who stayed back after Caesar was slain;
they resisted Caesar being dragged to the city square,
to be pelted with dead roses and iron shards;

waiting to be consoled for letting the wind past the doorway;
waiting to be charged for inflaming the skin under the chador –
for revealing crimped nipples, dead bulbuls, and a window
with lace curtains playing forbidden songs from childhood.

UNCHARTED

The Christmas toy for our fifteen-year-old is about new ways of dying.
Out the window, out in the wild, out in star haze, out in a train;
bloodstained pixels floating in farce. How simple is dying?

Don't ask Junaid. Alien gibber whacks, white, brown, black,
everyone's after blood. When did the killing start? It doesn't matter –
Just go, kick ass. That's what this is about. How hard is dying?

Don't ask Junaid. How hard – believing you were meant for dying?
How hard – feeling light fade from your eyes after you've been shot
or scythed. *How'd you know without trying?* There's faith in dying.

Is it all in the game – don't ask Junaid – how to zip down on the kill.
How to count down like a bomb in your breath, how to shoot and cover
before you go blind in the alley of blind. There's art in dying.

Running with friends, running past your kill, running like Junaid,
pellets in eyes, pushed under the train, running before you level up –
faster, running after you are dead. There's escape in dying.

The Christmas toy for our fifteen-year-old is about new ways of dying.
Out the window, out in the wild, out in star haze, don't ask Junaid –
tomorrow in a train, tomorrow in a game, there is heart in dying.

A FATHER'S REFLECTIONS UPON NAMING A CHILD

Walking by the ocean I find dog whelk buried in sand.
Inside, I hear winged ants building colonies of wax.
I want to ask the busker – what should I make of the song?

Anonymity is a place you travel and keep travelling, she says.
Even after you have lived enough and battled the storm
it remains a place. No busker will give away her song.

Stars that drilled through darkness a million years –
what do they care about the fat encyclopedia of skies?
Perhaps in their constant dying there's a method in the song.

The book of names they hand you, it has a million stories
glazed in sugar from wild dandelions. Will they stake a dagger
to your heart, if you turn to the junco for her song?

In the book of sounds you found a village; you found a well
covered in leaves, you found a forest, the sudden rush of fawn.
Why do you want to ask the cantor – what he made of the song?

Before there was mirror, before map and compass,
before the Ship of Theseus, before language and arithmetic,
go ask the ants what name they gave their song.

II. BELONGING

MUSKELLUNGE

A noisy hawfinch digs the pit out of a ripe plum;
hay bales cog the sky, a giant windmill turns; cows nod at the flies;
if you press your ear to the rock, you can hear the hum of porphyry.

When a fish tugs the bait, you want to be dead still;
when you see the snout raised and scales flashing under water,
you want to believe she is yours, ready to die.

When your head feels like it has taken off with the planes
and your toes are sore from gripping the shift, winding tackle
without thinking, fishing is an act of faith.

When you feel the soft fish-heart flapping inside your hands,
does it feel like soul? What follows epiphany is a kind of emptiness,
even though the sun on the Sturgeon entitles you.

Little water streams rise with the curve, crash.
The torque of the line guide pulls away, searching
pale yellow fingers in the upper sky. Fall is also about reminiscing.

You ease the fish off the hook expecting she'd turn around the rock.
You bend down on your knees expecting requite.
The sky is blue. Beavers never stop carting wood for their winter hold.

The fish has taken a piece of metal. Like a ring
noosed around a hurt, steeped in the dark silver of scales.
This is how we remember those who crossed our path? Not so the fish.

If you are fish, you sense the sun coming at you in waves,
everything touching everything; you know there is no dying;
nothing ever redeemed; no need for salvation.

ANECDOTE OF THE SPARROW

A white-throated sparrow
springs onto the edge of my bed –
drifts into the dream.

I grab her breast,
stroke her wings, underbelly, arteries –
she falls asleep.

I slide her into a camera,
through the dark sprockets, winding a spool
of film around her neck.

She lodges her head
at the rear of the curtain,
looks straight into the lens.

That's not the soul, she seems to say.
Her ruby eyes transfixed, legs beating –
Let me out!

Rewinding rollers,
I hold her close to the chest – almost secret.
I unfold the palm; she flies.

STRANGERS

Deep inside the trail where the gravel
tapers into the wild, when I hear voices –
must be them again, sharing joints, I think.
Turns out to be some stranger, grieving
over a landscape of dead nasturtiums.
She looks at me as though she knew
I too would come searching.

It's the end of day, and we search
for the half-moon upon the river,
thick with detritus and still vacillating
how exactly to fade away; rippled skin
around her eyes form into mounds
before gleaming, molten gold streams.
I don't know what she is grieving.

Fish, we think we can see them
streaked and striped in the afterlight,
as if they had done all the crying
and are ready to sleep, when I ask
if she can hear the madrones singing.
She shakes her head:
That's thunderclap, she says.

WALKING COOPER

Grass is dead. Leaves shuffle.
Ghosts gossip behind wet fronds of bougainvillea.

Someone has left a ladder full tilt, doing Christmas.
Sky is on slow burn; steel oats for breakfast.

Trees stand by shadows – dull lamps, terra-
cotta armies that stand and stand.

Someone's stabbing the snow exactly where the salt
has gorged a purple eye. The wind is a witch.

Squirrels in laundered tux walk like Beatles,
up and down the snow. Cooper breathes as if he knows.

A tin lobster looks down a high patio,
shiny with summer grease over a hooded stove.

The draft cuts through newsprint –
soggy deals, face-up on fences, a tube man with no limbs.

Walkers stride beneath smart hats, bursting galaxies.
Broken smiles heal beneath invisible slough.

Bobby's breakfast, churches, cemeteries and Lowe's
will soon claim all cars. Cooper breathes as if he knows.

ODE TO FORGETTING

In Detroit, right after a visit to Cole's,
distant view of Niagara Falls, we forget –
among the leaves – a hundred shades of yellow,
some harlequin, between bursts of rosewood –
where the car is parked.

In September's electric blue, we forget clouds
in the corners, with clots in their brain.
Rows upon rows of maple, birch and fern
vanish into a hospice bench where the pale shadow
of a man slouches toward a plaited head –
his daughter's. Forgotten.

The wind beats hard; a few stars have popped.
Squirrels have left the park to woodchucks.
The man looks into the void, his grey head so still,
you would think he has exhausted the need for breathing.
Bird calls vanish into the crimson.

His frail fingers dig into the hand resting on his lap.
A long time after twilight, in the far corner,
shadows fall off the cliff in flocks of thousands –
rising southward, toward the lake
the colour of cinnamon, almost curlew
and formed like a question.

OUTSIDE ST. ANN ELEMENTARY

Roads painted in gold, children
in cornrows, pigtails, twists, heading to school –
their bags have taken over the curb.

Weaves and spikes, braids and beads, strutting
in twos 'n' fours, past orange crossing guards
who have brought the world to stop.

Heads slinking out of coats, toy ghosts
in borrowed masks, descended to steal nectar
from the bees' secret haunts; their slim shoulders

flap away. Up there, aspens slam shut, then open.
The world grinds again into the square peg,
rapped by a sharp chill, blowing half green.

CLEARWATER

Pelicans, like pundits,
draw you into the curve of their pouch
quietly chewing carp – under your feet
sand shifts, as though earth were adjusting in sleep.
The clear green haze on the Atlantic
leaps up your body, begging to be touched.

Jaws slackened, pelicans sit still
watching the world – language of men,
depth of ocean – painted in bold white paint
on a weathered post – the sky
so brilliant, you wish you could squeeze
it to arouse your tongue.

Pelicans quietly chew before they take off,
all of them at once, before you notice –
ferrules on stretched umbrellas
creamed skin splayed under the sun
dreaming in shades of brown – men waving martinis
from shiny yachts and children drawing sand
in plastic buckets to build the castles
they know they can't take anywhere.

ODE TO OTHER WORLDS

Hummers are fighting for the yard –
their hearts beating a thousand;
maybe they will come back hungry as ever;
so what, if the feeder's empty.

The butterflies are gone.
Down the ravine, coyotes howl all night,
complaining: they feel, don't understand.
The skunks are out, digging new holes

under the dwarf blue spruce to make out,
while a dead maple, cut in pieces and stowed
at the edge of the wood with dead rock tripe
and winter green, has thrown all its secrets

out to the world in dark spinal rings:
Here, make of it what you want,
it seems to say, as if evangelizing the crows
breaking off twigs for their probes.

STILL THURSDAY

Holding the clammy hand of my six-year-old,
I am hoping for a miracle cheque from an estranged sister
in another continent.
He complains about a poke in his eye at school.

At the community mailbox, I find instead, a letter of recall
from the meat plant just two towns away in Troy.
I look up into the late-September sky. The beauty
of his deep brown eyes unspools as if it were waiting.

In the shrill screech of the bright green truck,
in the precise movements of the loader, throwing trash
into the gaping steel mouth, shadows of empty recycling bins
lengthen in twilight's slant and everything makes sense.

RACING A STORM

A blizzard is heading your way,
hailstones big as golf balls
wrecking homes, cars
in Columbus.
Go home!

The radio crackles.
Mind races storm – to Madrid – twenty years ago.
A bullfight after a day in museums.
Toreros amble into the arena: the bull's majestic walk;
gallop of the picador, glint of the lance
before it stabs the muscle mound
behind the bull neck.

Cars gone, the road's empty.
Maggots feed on a deer carcass by the shoulder.
The economy has tanked.
The storm is coming. Go home!

The best thing about Madrid –
Oh! Halved tomatoes will tell you of truths you only half know –
the way she said it – bulge of the purple tongue,
lips pursed, breath oaked with Merlot –
before the vinegar and the gall and crucifixion.

Outside, clouds come in rugged and silver
as if made of steel wool and slough.
A wafery blue moon on spring's Ohio skies,
heading north – a hummingbird
flies backwards over wrens locked in love.

Cows carry on, unmindful of infernos:
never bending to the wind,

never stopping to see what's passing.
Their bells ring as they shuffle.

Go home!
The radio crackles. Storm's
coming.

ODE TO STONE

You are the metal in my bones.
I see you in lemon-toned mornings
cutting through the window
and in heartless accents on the
red cement floor
and in the alphabet of rain
swirling like sea glass
near the window's border
where the sky leaps past the void

and in the speculum
on duck wings pointing
to the fisted sun
trying to survive the steel
wool of clouds

and in the stillness of the lake –
in its doomed iridescence
between weed and detritus
and in the black-eyed oriole
walking on water
conjoining shadows
inside the heart of lotus
the silk of spiderwebs

and in the smoke
on the other end of sky
layering everything
and in the fire
on the other side of sky
occasionally rising
and in the windowless huts
stood up on stilts in the bed of shit.

ODE TO RITUAL

Maurice Bloch says ritual is. Just talk.
Clifford Geertz says politicians make up rituals
to build their own pyramids of puff.
Edmund Leash says rituals save nations from epidemic incest.
Do you really care?

Life is either an ode or an elegy.
Who said what? You need food. Work.
If it's June, you take Felch through James
to Roosevelt and Centennial by Ben's Bookstore on 104th;
Ben'd be out in the sun dipping biscotti
in Turkish; that's ritual.

If July, Felch'd be all dug up, fines doubled,
and you'd be speeding to the beats of Glass. You'd take
Riley through 120th past Creekside Middle;
Dorothy's flowers? Pretty, but the boss is allergic to fragrances –
orchids are fine, but today is Wednesday.

Late August? DeBoer's'd be giving away doughnuts to anyone
ready to stick Hurricane Holland to their car bumper –
you take Douglas through James and back east,
to Centennial, past the Danish bakery –
free doughnuts mixed with the smell of rain.

That's ritual, like the torque on the soul – especially guilt
when you take Quincy in September up north through 120th
and back south to Centennial on 96th past the country steeple –
quaint letterboxes, opaque glass windows, bric-a-brac,
grey skies, hobble bush gone wild.

Today the air is thick as a noose
hanging head down on the lake as if dead.
Your black sedan cutting the lanes like a blade

past the red Corvette.
Ritual? Look 'em up again –
what's Glen doing under a Shantung fedora
letting you drive past? It's not yet Friday.

Perhaps he's talking to someone at the turn of sixteen,
perhaps the daughter who tried the ritual
of meth last December,
perhaps weekend sororities always end in blood,
now to dopamine and dopamine,
now to deep sleep and deep sleep.

NEW HOMES

In this commercial, I am running.
Running is art. I have been at it.
I don't know how long –
from emerald to chartreuse on their way to gold–
larch and junipers and aspen: they are still.
Leaves so brilliant, it hurts to look at them.
Birds stream out of leaves so blinded
they shoot straight at me.

Birdsong in the trees as I run,
on a möbius strip, for this commercial;
among used utensils wrapped in cardboard on the curb;
between white and orange marks on pavements,
past walls, fences, sprinklers, skin, the smell of cut grass;
dull shine on shut garage doors.

On the far end there's river;
maybe to the river I am running;
on the other side there's woods
reflected in the river.

Stones stick out of driveways,
weeds scrunched between stones; words between thoughts;
birdsong climbing the steeple before a mad chorus.
Still I am running.

The feel of my heart pumping – piston in every muscle –
sweat bursting like stars; the feel of the song's bridge
taking over the coda – in a flash,
synched with the switch at the stop sign;
the feel of lungs grasping twilight, skin glazed in pollen,
eyes outshining traffic, bleeding in the dark.
In this commercial, I am back at the start,
inside my closed fist: Śūnyatā.

AFTER A WEEK IN COLLEGE: PHILOSOPHY

Experience:
At a hardware store
looking for a lip for the broken plate on the door bolt –
I realize how much depends on those fingers:
unsure in the act of sitting a cherry on the chin cleft;
peeling the dark, before unravelling the head bun.

Choice:
Sunday. I am in a temple.
A committee of elders explains the rituals of dying.
But I am helpless, battling a wicked flutter
inside my eyes, created by a blue butterfly
inked on the naked shoulder blade of a congregant
sitting ahead of me, sweat glazed on her swan nape.

Meaning:
At the parking lot outside a train station, I make sure
the dink on the car door is actually dimpled sun.
Inside the train, I hear language spoken in multiple tongues
caressing a chorography of scars,
soothed and shut by the morpheme of vowels.

Reality:
He says the switch to her peach fuzz
hides in her earlobes; she likes the kisses dry;
he likes her hair brushed back and shining,
reminds him of a teacher in grade school
who touched him; she doesn't like
to be touched in the bath; he doesn't
like the aftertaste of sleep.

God:
On a wintry afternoon, snow feeds the wood rot
on the ledge; red and white streams of amaryllis
speckle the window; shadow of maple
sprawls between a squirrel's footprints,
reveals the sun. Someone arranged the stage.

Morality:
An accountant who owns a church explains
the dominion of the golden rule: you do unto others...
But how does one know if it's more right
to go with the coital pulse or worry about the hurt?
You judge it from the sound, he says.

Afterlife:
I try reasoning with the public prosecutor,
why red-light cameras don't always provide the whole picture.
What if you weren't here to explain? she asks.
After dying, at least I'd hope not to experience a whiplash
of spider bites; stiffness of soul;
this despairing otherness inside the gristle.

TIN AQUARIUM

What do silver sharks in tin aquariums care
whether they are scaling oceans?
When they look through the glass reliquary
do they see reflection or shadows framed in light?

What do silver sharks in tin aquariums care
about a sea god covered in plastic moss spewing
missives they must obey no more
than the sun shining like an electric bulb?

What do silver sharks in tin aquariums care
about windmills, or the pearls, bloated
from eating their own dreams, like some saint
watching her own flesh glow inside a vase?

Sun on their back tuned to instinct,
perhaps they hear the water singing a different song.
What do silver sharks in tin aquariums care
who among them is fish, who's worm or krill?

TRENT HILL

On my way to Trent Hill
someone sits facing me in the train – speaking
into her phone a strange patois, occasionally looking out.

I think of her the whole time:
why must all her words end in diphthongs?
What makes her hair that peculiar red?

Sun breaks down in pauses as if making a point
about something important. Quaint houses
dance with the wind reflected on a mirror lake.

I sit looking and wondering.
What am I doing here in this sun-washed afternoon
so dazzling I must wake myself again and again?

Rows upon rows of grapes wait for spring;
fog winds around leafless branches of ash
like a lover aroused but nervous.

The shape of a frozen stream in the sun
like the girl's unmindful shoulder blade, chiselled
as she bends over to rebut, reclaim.

The stilts of bridges – uneven and weathered
like teeth – afraid they will have to let go,
release us from this oppressive beauty.

What do we really see when we see?
Was that hemlock by the bridge?
What was the girl across from me asking?

What if there isn't an afterlife?
How long will this beauty matter before fear takes over?
Can she disembark at her station, come back at will?

FAITH HEALER FEEDING FIGS

When I saw Dr. M, he was still washing
his hands off the last visitant.
What do you want? he said.
Happiness. Fulfilment. Rest.
I am tired, I said.
Show me your right hand, he said;
I am carpal tunnelled, I said.
I can't hold it out long without pain,
but my left hand is strong.
What's a little pain? he said,
his eyes piercing the fade of a wry smile.
Do you have a natal chart? he said.
I can't have one, I said.
Why not? Everyone is born
at least once, he said.
I was found, abandoned
outside a city dumpster, wrapped in plastic, I said.
Wait, he said, rising from his desk.
He took out a silver case filled with ash.
Take a pinch; throw it here, he said,
pointing at the floor.
As he sat examining fractals on the black granite,
it seemed like an ancient ritual I should have known.
When I looked up,
he had escaped his body: eyes shut,
on shadow candles and floating amaryllis.
Take this, he said, holding out a dried fig
from a wooden bowl on the left.
What's that? I said.
He didn't answer.
Now face the sky, he said,
pointing to a shut window.
Feel the sun erupting inside your eyes,
don't stop the fig, let it flow.

Feel it travelling in sunburst.
Now feel the fig settle around your feet,
feel it shooting up your body,
reaching the solar plexus.
Now feel your feet. So heavy.
Now feel your head towering outside.
Now you are a tree.
I threw it right back at him.
Enough, I said –
my feet heavy, light-headed for real,
as if I had stepped into a glue trap.
I shook with anger, betrayal, despair.
Don't you want it? he said.
What? I said.
Happiness. Fulfilment. Rest?
No. No. No, I said.

WINTER BIRDS

slouched on fence caps
like chickadees weaving their requiem
for the dead to stay where they are

a red patch in the gessoed canvas
is the crest of the Christmas tie
moving like a crank, at an angle

the mind of the alder – gashed open
the mind of the woodpecker – unyielding
as if it were a game and they knew each other.

III. DEATH

ODE TO A BROKEN ELM

April: the squirrels are between maples
with a new coat of paint.
Gladiolas, hobblebush, dogwood and rockets
have gathered around an ancient elm
broken since December, at the base of the trunk,
as if it were some price you pay
to the old spirit at Staghorn Copse.

Everyone knows it's here.
Nothing escapes it.
You can tell from the calm after-squall:
unmoving eyelids, awake to every move;
a million peepers peering
down the low lintel of loopy mirrors –
newborn and hungry for sun.

By the feet of the broken elm –
parts that were once heartwood –
those parts are marked in orange,
to be cast to flame or perhaps
into quaint tables to hold the aquarium.

Meanwhile, field ants have gathered.
Blanched leaves fold themselves
down to the size of cracks
in the dirt below,
trying to re-enter, reincarnate.

MY MOTHER'S BRAIN

Like a sky where fractals of dead
stars have left in their wake
signs of being –
yes, she was happy
watching the dahlias.

Yet that's not quite
the whole story.

Like the picture of my mother's brain –
now battling to make out red,
what got captured on the film –
held out shakily against
the filtered sun of an unremarkable
afternoon – is just an aspect,
not quite the story.

No. She was no longer angry;
she had no more regrets.
And it was just the fact
of finding the rounded nub,
hung like a pendant she needed to press;
just the fact of not remembering –
she hated to call for help.

ODE TO A BURNING MAPLE

This fall the maples have said no
to fear. Nothing can scare
them out of their gold trappings.

Others have quietly yielded:
judases, sycamores, tupelos –
They're done ghosting around

the chicken fence,
between grass blades, inside brown bags.
They are ready to zero down again.

The birds are gone. Naked
branches slither under the moon,
empty pythons wrestling wind. Alone, out

of step, the maples burn –
bright halo over shaggy heads,
blue-black inside veins, resisting
what seems inevitable.

Burn as though they had something important
to prove, pass on –
more than fear or revenge, meaning;
desire to make a difference here.

BOUQUET FROM BINGO

It's May – moths blinded by sunset
dash into the glass window as if
they were schooled to die elegantly.

In hospice, a mother recovers from a heart attack.
Sons in dapper suits press her hands, whisper.
Daughters-in-law stay at a distance.

What are they saying?
Is there something the dying must know or say?
What good is knowing before the end?

White tube roses shine inside a cellophaned bouquet,
From Bingo...Bingo,
she commands her larynx to repeat.

There is no voice; her mouth freezes in an O.
Lilies bend under their own weight, dissolving
in a green haze – the water inside the vase is yellow.

On the wall, clock hands join in a namaste.
Everyone's gone. Cicadas will take over soon.
The closed window will burst with stars.

SEVEN ODES TO DYING

I

Lungs clogged with dragon tar;
nurses exhausted, pumping the inhaler;
my father was often breathless
but never short of ghosts –
the four-eyed-dog licking my feet.
He said, drawing on the muscles
around his upper lip,
one last time,
like a torero
preparing his final duel.
He knew he wasn't immortal.
Sometimes he had doubts.
Come on, bring what you got.
He said, or seemed to say,
with a swift flow of fingers.
He had lost his voice.
He'd ask for time
whenever someone passed him,
never for the verdict.
If someone stopped,
he'd grasp the hand tight, say nothing.

2

My mother,
numbed in that part of the brain
that connects to the mirror
reflecting past lives
silent behind our eyes
in the pool
between pink lilies,
and little redfish
flying off craggy pumice stones;
where the soul walks naked
and saws the calluses;
pushed to the sharp edge,
she walked the razor moment,
sutured to a window by the sink.
Stealing away late,
after the nurses were gone,
rocking the gurney,
she looked at a distance.

3

When morning arrived –
Call your mother, my father gestured,
as if he had something urgent to record.
Mother walked in and out of the room,
barely breathing, barely looking.
Her arms clasped in her hands,
hair hanging down her back,
head knocking on things;
then back to the escape hatch –
the window by the sink.
What he was thinking, who knows.
There were other things –
a strapped leather valise that wouldn't close;
unwritten wills, unpaid testaments;
a pair of glasses he accidentally broke.

4

Midnight, the wheezing stopped.
So what if we knew?
So what if we were ready?
I pressed at his misshapen wrists,
unsure if it was his nerve
or my memory of him
throbbing against the spiderweb of hope.

He stared as though he wanted to disgorge,
with his razor tongue,
the final words stuck in the velum.

What more did he have to say?

He thought nothing about confessions.
He never believed in atonement.
He never thought death was a place.

Have you ever looked at moth wings
splayed on wild bindweed?
What does that mean?
Have you ever seen a snake eating its tail?
What does *that* mean?

5

At the end we needed air.
Trudging up food-smudged stairways
to the terrace, I could feel the brain –
the slow ticking of a bomb
wired to a tin box –
the sound of loss and synapsis.

I wasn't hallucinating.

Heaven or what, I couldn't tell –
but it was a steep climb at a sharp angle.

A kind of departure.
Someone said, *Look*.
And I looked.
Down on the pavement, people slept
as if they had memorized the weather
and mastered the art
of lucid dreaming.

6

What do we talk of when we talk of death?

Up there
someone tapped on the rain-jarred balustrade;
a piece of mortar flew off the latticework
sharp-edged like a rapier;

it fell past the fig tree,
smashed the windshield of a parked sedan.

The woman down the street
still dresses in dark cloaks
and her husband still reads palms,
fits stones into voids left open
by erasures.

Then we talked about rain.

7

After the fire we walked the pocked beach
and shoved the urn into the river's red eye.
The ashes drowned instantly
before buoying back up, wet.
Mother said, *Those are ghosts,*
pointing at the shimmy
of shadows in tamarind trees.

Come to me, Mother had heard them say.

Where exactly they wanted her to follow
she never revealed, nor settled for
anything less than complete surrender
to her sense of knowing.

We followed her,
failing to keep up in the sand.
Her stare split open,
we folded under her wings,
flapping over invisible stairways of ritual.

It was hard to breathe at that height.

The sky lay flat over steel and concrete.
A yellow crane planted red girders deep inside the dark.
Further up, smog sat like a hijab,
stifling everything said, not said.

A fire stretched across the other side of the river.
Nothing ever just happens, she said,
holding on to her cape.

FRESH TULIPS IN VASE

After the guests were gone –
past thumbprints on used wineglasses –
fresh-cut tulips in a vase
held the lemon sun, like water
inside a cupped palm.

How time moves, why religion fails,
how hate hangs in corners and ledges;
what cuts us down to the bone, instincts
we claim and deny, the tulips seemed to know.
They live outside the shrapnel of time.

We barely spoke during winter.
The first wrinkles showed around the edges
of the upper lip, then in the hollow of throat,
then in the back of neck, then under eye bags.
Wrinkles like moon water seeping under shine.

Once radiant, now lucid
like butterflies pinned to the popcorn
wall around the terracotta vase – winter light
shot upward, before falling off the ceiling joist
as though it were scared of heights.

MOMENTS BEFORE ICE SHATTERS ROOF

A foot away, the terrace,
then the lake gone quiet –
the kind of blue-green you feel
inside the lip of mussel.
It's bright out and the long coats
flap as if they have been
let off leash today.
Seaweed-green tarps on parked boats
prattle on the near end,
playing back to the wind
whatever the wind wants to hear;
rocking forward in respect,
ready to fly past the pier,
before stopping to reflect, as if
the water was hiding something.

The red stern of a lone boat
sits on the lake's frozen face
like a zit you want to pop
without thought, plain instinct.
Like the last Mughal poet,
you want to soak the world in blood
and effulgence, as if it were a bad tumour,
this conscious life,
always threatening to end.

Then you want to believe in promise –
things that can be started again;
a whole new state of being;
not the same as naming,
today you have no need for naming.
The weathervane spins.
You know there is no one here
to stop you from roiling

past the flaking paint on the guardrails;
nothing holding you back from taking in
the wind with a straight face,
going down.

What difference does it make –
separating papaya whip
from fuchsia in the fallen sassafras?

You know you'd miss the sailboat
the moment it's gone.
How much?
How to sense the hurt of fall
if you haven't fallen?
You don't know until a slice of crusted snow
breaks out the latticework,
as if this was well-rehearsed –
as if this has happened before –
the edge of crusted ice takes in the sun,
going down like a dagger into the umbilicus.

The second it lands
the dull glass dome shatters.
You don't know for a fact
if it was ice that broke before the glass
or the geysers trapped inside.
You just know the Flower Girls
are not going to like that.

STAGES TO FORGETTING

Sometime later,
you know,
there are stages to forgetting.

Keys, then words; names; faces, colours:
kinds of purple –
plum, periwinkle, boysenberry?

There is a bird on the feeder – orange like cut papaya.
Is the bird singing? Or longing?
Is the bird from here? Or flown
a thousand miles just to pay back debts?

Who will return what's owed to her?
How would she get home?

When you say birds have maps and clocks
in their heart, she simply turns away,
her chin pointed toward the closed window,
as if searching for the right word –

I believe you.
Or perhaps – *Why should I believe you?*
Did you pay back the debt?

SPECULATIONS ABOUT SOUL

On my way to see my mother –
still in her early stages of forgetting –
I met a beekeeper off to seek from a guru
an understanding of soul.

For a brief period, it was perfect.
Until she showed me
how she was once held
by the neck, down on her knees,
forced to find her soul
in her own reflection inside
a glass bowl filled with water.

That's it!

Seeing her soul reflected in still water
made her think about herself
as a water poppy, floating
with a halo around the whetted edge
bursting out in entelechy, her opiate eyes
like bulbs, luminous where the sun
couldn't penetrate

the dark of the glass held together by water –
the dark of the water peeled down
in abstract mishmash of shadows, spread
unevenly with no respect for unity,
borders – everything in everything.
Petals of poppy heads breaking form –
becoming ghosts.
Elegant.
Unrooted. Unmoored.

"That's it?"

By evening, as the woods closed in
and the high windows dissolved into
coyotes calling out for love,
she became sick with guilt
getting so close to knowing,
before the shock remorse –
"What if I've been tricked?"

Like animals bent over a glass bowl,
we sat on our haunches, concentrating
on a mould stain beneath our floating holograms.
Then we were yelling obscenities
at the shape-shifting Grendelesque thing –
a different kind of soul.
She said she heard the howl
when she poked.

Could have been the grass we'd smoked
or the bat song some hear at certain frequencies.
We made love just so we could shift
the weight of consciousness
from shadow to skin, like a needle threading
back into form, as if it were rite of passage.

Barely lucid, our senses slipping –
we lay side by side like empty pillboxes,
in this new religion we had accidentally found,
aching to reach the limit –
as if it were a sign of a fresh start
when we are left with an aftertaste
and a craving.

NOTES

"The Mutating Life of Symbols" – Refers to "swastika," derived from Devanagari "swastika," a symbol of health, luck, success, prosperity; hand-drawn with vermillion on walls in every room at my Calcutta home, where I spent the first ten uninterrupted years of my life.

"Crouching Cavemen Hidden Cellar" – Alludes to Richard Krantz's felt-tip-pen-and-ink on paper *The World's First Patriot*.

"Muskellunge" – Inspired by and in response to Elizabeth Bishop's "A Tremendous Fish."

"Song of Aylan" – Dedicated to Aylan Kurdy, 2012–15.

"Uncharted" – Junaid Khan was stabbed and thrown out of a running train in Northern India, allegedly by a group of Hindu zealots after a dust-up over seats. He was fifteen.

ACKNOWLEDGEMENTS

Many thanks to the editors of the journals where these poems first appeared, sometimes in different forms:
Canadian Literature: "Maria after the Concert"
Contemporary Verse 2: "My Grandma's Virgin"
Crosswinds: "History Lesson at School"
Eastlit Journal: "Still Thursday" and "The Broken Elm"
Eunoia: "Fresh Tulips in Vase"
Emerge18: "How to Raise Them in Moss Park," "Strangers," and "Things You Do Racing a Storm"
Grain: "On Forgetting"
One Sentence Poems: "Winter Birds"
Orbis: "How to Interpret a Dream"
River and South Review: "Clearwater"
r.kv.r.y. Quarterly: "Remedies for Tereusitis"

Squaw Valley Review: "About Reaching Centennial"
The Antigonish Review: "Dealing with the Witnesses"
The Dalhousie Review: "Walking Cooper"
The Maynard: "Catastrophe That Nearly Brought Down a Plane"
The Write Launch: "Crouching Caveman Hidden Cellar" and
    "Song of Aylan"
The Windsor Review: "What We Make of Symbols"
Vallum: "Burning Maple"

I am grateful to Betsy Warland, Carole Baldock, and Stella Harvey for their help with several poems included in this collection. Thanks to the Community of Writers at Squaw Valley, and in particular C. D. Wright, Don Mee Choi, Harryette Mullen, Matthew Zapruder, and Robert Hass for their help in the making of some of the poems. Thanks, Keka, for always being able to see things more clearly; thank you, Rishabh, for your quiet intelligence and sound insights. Deepest gratitude to Denis De Klerck of Mansfield Press; thank you, Stuart Ross, for your generous reading and insightful edits; and to friends and colleagues who supported this collection with their encouragement, ideas, and inspiration.

Sabyasachi Nag (Sachi) is the author of two previous collections of poetry: *Bloodlines* (Writers Workshop, 2006) and *Could You Please, Please Stop Singing* (Mosaic Press, 2015). He is a graduate of the Writer's Studio at Simon Fraser University and Humber School for Writers. He lives in Mississauga, Ontario.